HEART SONGS

Poetry, Lyrics and Meditations
from across the years

Julie Hutchin

authorHOUSE®

AuthorHouse™ UK
1663 Liberty Drive
Bloomington, IN 47403 USA
www.authorhouse.co.uk
Phone: UK TFN: 0800 0148641 (Toll Free inside the UK)
UK Local: (02) 0369 56322 (+44 20 3695 6322 from outside the UK)

© 2024 Julie Hutchin. All rights reserved.

No part of this book may be reproduced, stored in a retrieval system, or transmitted by any means without the written permission of the author.

Published by AuthorHouse 07/23/2024

ISBN: 979-8-8230-8874-9 (sc)
ISBN: 979-8-8230-8875-6 (e)

Library of Congress Control Number: 2024914287

Print information available on the last page.

Any people depicted in stock imagery provided by Getty Images are models, and such images are being used for illustrative purposes only. Certain stock imagery © Getty Images.

This book is printed on acid-free paper.

Because of the dynamic nature of the Internet, any web addresses or links contained in this book may have changed since publication and may no longer be valid. The views expressed in this work are solely those of the author and do not necessarily reflect the views of the publisher, and the publisher hereby disclaims any responsibility for them.

Contents

1. Hebrews 2:14,15 1
2. Sovereign Love 2
3. I Bow to the Mystery 3
4. Resting 4
5. Lord, You Have Searched Me 5
6. Prayer to the Father 6
7. Like a Lover 7
8. From Broken Places 8
9. Chosen by God 9
10. This is My Body 10
11. Hidden Treasures 11
12. Open My Eyes 12
13. Make Me a Channel 13
14. Hungry 14
15. Rescued 15
16. Carried 16
17. Prodigal 17
18. Loved 18
19. I Give My Heart 19
20. Hope 20
21. When Times are Difficult 21
22. Gentle In My Spirit 22
23. I Sing of Love 23
24. When I Fear 24
25. Through All the Years 25
26. Everlasting Arms 27
27. The Walled Garden 28
28. The Power of Your Love 30
29. Open My Eyes 31
30. There is a Place 32

31. Father 33
32. Judas 34
33. Broken World 35
34. Inspire 36
35. Reach Out 37
36. I Lift My Eyes 38
37. Here I Stand 39
38. When I Think 40
39. Perfect Love 41
40. Just Come 42

*Because God's children are human
beings made of flesh and blood,
the Son also became flesh and blood.
For only as a human being could he die, and only by
dying could he break the power of the one who had the
power of death - that is the Devil - and free those who all
their lives were held in slavery by their fear of death.*

Hebrews 2:14,15

Sovereign Love

Sovereign love who reigns in pain and majesty
What lips can true full tribute bring
No heart can plumb the depths of suffering
That you bore
to free us from captivity

Eternal love enthroned in Heaven and our hearts
Can we begin to understand?
The passion in Your heart, the fire that's burning there.
You gave yourself for love of man
Sovereign love.

Lord of creation who sustains us by your word
There is no other like you are
The courts of heaven now are ringing with your praise
We stand with them and bless your Name
Your lovely Name,
Jesus

"He is far above all rulers, authorities, powers, lords, and all other names that can be named, not only in this present world but also in the world to come." (Ephesians 1:21)

I Bow to the Mystery

I bow to the mystery of Majesty.
The God of creation who died for me.
There is no other deserving my praise.
There is no other deserving my gaze.

So in worship I am yielding my heart
With a song rising up from within
But my words are not enough
to magnify Your Name
So I offer up my life again
I offer up my life again.

For Your beauty, for Your glory
I join in heaven's praise
For Your love so precious and true
For the life that You have given
And the power of Your Name
Jesus, I worship You

I bow to the mystery of Majesty
The God of creation who died for me
There is no other deserving my praise
There is no other deserving my gaze.

"Therefore, God has highly exalted Him, and has given Him a name which is above every name." (Philippians 2:9)

Resting

I'm resting Lord
My heart now quiet before You
With everything in Your hands.
Knowing Your peace
Just wanting to adore You
For all that You understand

I'm resting Lord
You have my heart again
With everything it contains.
Secure in You
Knowing Your love again
Washing away all my stains.

You are my safe place
I will abide in the comfort of Your arms
And I will hide in the shelter of Your wings.
You make me sing.

You are the strength of my life
You are my rock when I'm tossed by the storm
You give me wings and I fly
Into Your presence and there I am singing....

"Come to me all you who are weary and heavy laden and I will give you rest." (Matthew 11:28)

Lord, You Have Searched Me

(Based on Ps 139)

Oh Lord, You have searched me
You have known me from the start.
Even before my life had begun, You were there.
Oh Lord, You have made me.
You formed me in the womb.
In secret You created all I am
I'm part of Your plan.

I am fearfully and wonderfully made
In Your image – for Your glory.
And my heart sings for joy
At the knowledge that You love me.

Oh Lord, it's a mystery
Just why my life began.
But it's enough to know that You care,
And my life is in Your hands.
Oh Lord, why should I worry
About the many things I don't understand.;
You are so much bigger than all
I can see or comprehend.

You're the One who is the start
And the ending of all things – the Creator.
And the peace which is so overwhelming
Comes from knowing You.
I want to know You Lord,
And love you more.

Prayer to the Father

"Heavenly Father, help me to not feed on my failings or fearfulness, but to nourish myself on Your faithfulness and goodness."

"A joyful heart makes the face cheerful, but heartache crushes the spirit." (Proverbs 15:13)

Like a Lover

Here I am LORD
Sitting at your feet
Longing to hear your voice
Longing to hear you speak

The world outside this place
Can nothing offer me
It is your presence that I long for
It is your presence that I seek

Like a lover now I run into your arms
In the secret place my heart
  is knit with yours
To know you LORD is all that I desire
Come touch me now
Set my heart on fire.

"...and Mary sat at the feet of Jesus" (Luke 10:39)

From Broken Places

From broken places you have lifted me
From dark alleyways of wandering
Drawn me deeper into Your light
I'm enveloped in Your mercy

Precious Healer, You have rescued me
Made a treasure from my wounded heart
You have found me and surrounded me
With singing, now and forever

Carried by your love
On wings of joy I rise in freedom
Now I have Your peace
I am strong to face the storms.

You are my promise
My promise keeper
I will never be alone again
You are forever and unchanging
with a love that never ends.
It never ends

"The righteous call to the LORD, and he listens; he rescues them from all their troubles." (Psalm 34:17)

"Now we know that all things work together for good for those who love God, who are called according to His purpose." Romans 8:28

Chosen by God
From "The Life Giver" musical

Chosen by God
But by all men forsaken
Lifted up high on a cross made of wood
Hands that once healed
Cruelly nailed, torn and bleeding
Eyes that once shone
Filled with blood.

"King of the Jews"
Is the name they have given him
Mocking and scorning
Without any shame
Yet there's no king in the earth
Or his splendour
As matchless in beauty
As his beaten frame.

This is My Body

From "The Life Giver" musical

This is my body broken for you
Take eat, all of you
This is my blood poured out for you
Take drink, all of you

This is my covenant of love
Remember me
Forgiving all you're guilty of
Remember me, remember me

"For He made Him who knew no <u>sin</u> to be sin for us, that we might become the righteousness of God in Him." (<u>2 Corinthians 5:21</u>)

Hidden Treasures

Day by day we are watching on TV and Facebook inspiring stories of creativity and courage.

This reminds me of a wonderful verse in the Bible, *"I will give you hidden treasures, riches stored in secret places, so that you may know that I am the LORD ….," (Isaiah 45:3)*

There are many forces at work in our world that bring us into dark places. Sometimes our own mistakes, or the actions of others, and even nature itself that the Bible says groans to be set free from its decay (Romans 8:21).

Yet in all we see and all that we experience, God is at work, deeply involved and working to transform every situation into an opportunity to triumph, if we will let Him.

There are hidden treasures to be found, new experiences, new depth of understanding, and also the opportunity to draw close to God and deepen, or discover, our faith.

"It is the Lord who goes before you. He will be with you; he will not leave you or forsake you. Do not fear or be dismayed." (Deuteronomy 31:8)

"Some of us are always looking for opportunities to put ourselves down while God is looking for opportunities to raise us up!"

Open My Eyes

Open my eyes LORD
That I may see
The truth in your word
That is setting me free

Open my ears LORD
Cause me to hear
Your whispers of love to me
When I draw near

Make Me a Channel

Make me a channel of your love
Touch my life and make it beautiful
May the sunshine of your smile
Light up the corners of my heart

Make me a channel of your love
Oh, Lord, reach into every part of me
May someone else bathe in the glow
Of your love poured out in me
Your love in me

"Love never gives up; and its faith, hope, and patience never fail." (1Co 13:7)

"If we choose only to focus on the bad and refuse to honour what is good in someone, how can we expect God to honour the good that we do above all that is not?" (Matthew 7:1-5)

Hungry

I'm hungry Lord
I long for more of you
To know your will
In everything I do.
The things that used to please
No longer satisfy
Now I know the reason why.

Just like a child
Whose childish days are gone
I need to grow
To rise up and move on
There's so much more
I need to know, so much to do
And to discover about you.

I'm reaching higher Lord
I want to touch your throne
I know you've made a way
For me through grace alone
And in your presence
I can stand in faith complete
Again, I fall in love with you
and worship at your feet

"Blessed are they who hunger and thirst after righteousness! For they shall be filled." (Matthew 5:6)

Rescued

I sing of love that rescued me
I sing of love that never ends
Of One who gave His life for me
Who is my lover and my friend
There is no-one I could love more
It's He alone who holds my heart
And I will own for evermore
Jesus my Saviour and my God.

I sing of grace that covers me
Free flowing from the Father's heart
Grateful and captive I will be
Surrendered now in every part.
No-one has given me such worth
As He who'll love me to the end
And I will serve forevermore
Jesus my Saviour and my friend.

I sing of glory that's to come
Safe and victorious from the fight.
The splendour of my eternal home
Of power and majesty and might
Nothing will take my joy away
As I behold my God and King
And there for day on precious day
To Jesus I will always sing

"He rescued us from the domain of darkness and brought us into the kingdom of the Son whom He loves." (Col 1:13)

Carried

I carried you from before
You even knew My Name
Throughout the years, beside you,
And sharing all your pain

I bore your griefs and sorrows
Though you didn't see me there,
When you sat in loneliness,
Believing no-one cared

In the hidden places
My presence has been near
Ready to bring comfort
And challenge every fear

Always close and waiting
I hear the smallest prayer
When you reach out to find me
To know I really care

I am Alpha and Omega
Beginning and the end
Redeemer and Saviour
And your Eternal friend.
Jesus

(Exodus 19:4, Deuteronomy 8:2, Isaiah 53:4, Psalm 27:5, Psalm 34:18, Jeremiah 33:3, Revelation 1:8)

Prodigal

There's a place in my heart you left behind you
As you walked further down the road away from me
And the space that you left there is still hurting
All because I risked my love to keep you free

There is pain in your heart and I can feel it
All the waste of a lifetime spent in chasing dreams
But it's not enough to stop me loving you
And the way back is not as long as it may seem.

And every day my heart is breaking waiting for you
Every day I long that this day you will come
And every day I'm waiting here
Reaching out towards you saying,

"Forget those vain imaginings
Forsake your lonely wanderings
Remember me and come on home."

From the story of the prodigal son. (Luke 15:11-22)

Loved

"You have loved my soul
out of the pit of destruction!
For you have flung all my sins
behind your back."

(Isaiah 38:17b)

I Give My Heart

I give my heart
LORD, I give my heart to you
In the presence of your love
Laying down my life in thankfulness
For all you've given me

Deep rivers from inside
Wash over and release me
from my shame
You make me clean
I speak your name

And in your peace
Fear and doubt can find no room
With tomorrow in your hands
Hands that once were stretched out
In sacrificial love

Heaven has descended
And filled my feeble heart
With endless grace
I rise renewed
To follow you
I give my heart

"For where your treasure is, there your heart will be also."
(Matthew 6:21)

Hope

There is a hope. There is a future
There is a life beyond the cross
He's gone before us
Our great deliverer
To give us victory
Over every loss

And we may suffer and know sorrow for a night
But day is dawning into everlasting light

So we will stand. We will fight
We will say we are the Lord's
And lift the Name of Jesus high
We'll be strong In His might
He has overcome all evil
And our victory is in sight
We will stand

There is a promise
A word from Heaven
We know His Word will never fail
Mighty in power
His love will conquer
His grace and mercy will prevail.

So we will stand…….

"We have this hope as an anchor for the soul, firm and secure." (Hebrews 6:19)

When Times are Difficult

In these difficult days that we are in right now, it seems that it is really important for us to know that we are not here by accident. Each of us has been born for such a time as this and by God's design. This means that you and I have a place in His purposes. The world may seem out of control, but God is not! He has a plan for each of our lives that has been in His heart since before each of us was born.

This means we are already equipped through Christ to meet the challenges that lie before us. God is our Provider, our Healer, the One who empowers us and gives us strength for every day. His resources are limitless, His power infinite and His love unwavering.

As we give our lives to Him daily, we find that He works in wonderful and surprising ways even in the darkest places. As a result, our lives shine brighter so that others see the light and are drawn to experience Jesus for themselves.

"For he chose us in him before the creation of the world to be holy and blameless in his sight. In love he predestined us for adoption to sonship through Jesus Christ, in accordance with his pleasure and will.." (Ephesians 1:4,5)

"Peace, I leave with you. My peace I give to you. I do not give as the world gives. Do not let your hearts be troubled and do not be afraid." (John 14:27)

Gentle In My Spirit

Just a few quiet minutes LORD
To tell you how I feel
Everything you've done for me
Is so beautiful and so real
You're King of all the universe
Of all life you are the source
So, ask me why I love you
I love you because

You're so gentle in my spirit
Whispering softly in my ear
Sometimes I feel the warm glow
Of your presence when you're near
Peaceful in my thinking
Patient with my pride
So tender in your Father love
Yet mighty on my side

Father there's so many times
I've worked things out my way
Yet you wait so patiently
Until I've had my say
and knowing what a fool I've been
You never put me down
But lead me into victory
And promise me a crown.

"… for I am gentle and humble in heart, and you will find rest for your souls." (Matthew 11:29}

I Sing of Love

I sing of love that rescued me
I sing of love that never ends
Of One who gave His life for me
Who is my lover and my friend
There is no-one I could love more
It's He alone who holds my heart
And I will own for evermore
Jesus my Saviour and my God.

I sing of grace that covers me
Free flowing from the Father's heart
Grateful and captive I will be
Surrendered now in every part.
No-one has given me such worth
As He who'll love me to the end
And I will serve forevermore
Jesus my Saviour and my friend.

I sing of glory that's to come
Safe and victorious from the fight.
The splendour of my eternal home
Of power and majesty and might
Nothing will take my joy away
As I behold my God and King
And there for day on precious day
To Jesus I will always sing

"Therefore, He is also able to save completely those who draw near to God through Him, always living to make intercession for them." (Hebrews 7:25)

When I Fear

So many scenes surround me
Sad scenes that at are there before my eyes
Lord you see them
The world seems caught in madness
It's so hard to find a happy ending
But Lord You know

Yet when I fear, it's then You draw near to my heart.
You give me your Word, your strength is assured
To every trembling part

When I am afraid, I'll put my trust in You
I'll call out Your Name
I know that Your Word is true,
Your love will carry me through
I'll put my trust in You

You give my life direction
You're the One who's the anchor in my storms
I love to be near You
I'll rest in Your perfection
No-one else can hold me like You do
Your love is so strong!

Open my eyes, help me to see Your grace
Lift up my heart, cause me to sing
Your praises in this place

"When I am afraid, I will put my trust in you." (Psalm 56:3)

Through All the Years

Lord, you were my help in all years past
And even now you are.
You are the same, you have not changed.
You do not stand afar

My closest friend My confidence
In whom my hope still rests
You calm my fears You make a way
You draw me to Your breast.

When in darkness or confusion
Your light always shines
Yours is the truth that always stands
And will throughout all time

And on this rock, I'll always stand,
And on this rock alone.
Your promises, your faithfulness
Made mine through your own Son

Through His great love I have become
A treasure to your heart
Like a small child In Your embrace
I'll bring each troubled part

I am your child, always will be
Through all eternity
My Lord, my God, my Father still.
Your love, it comforts me.

"During times of trouble I called on the LORD. The LORD answered me and set me free from all of them." (Psalm 118:5)

Everlasting Arms

When trouble overcomes me
And faith is faltering in the trial
LORD, I know you are there
And when I'm weak and weary
With no more strength to face the day
I can trust in your care
For you are faithful and true
And no one loves me the way that you do

Underneath me are your everlasting arms
Your raise me up and draw me close to your heart
You are my security I need not be alarmed
Whatever happens I am safe in your love

When peace escapes me and my thoughts
Are restless and disturbed
You have promised your calm
When tears have stained my pillow
And loneliness comes creeping in
I am not on my own
For you are faithful and true
And no one loves me the way that you do

"The eternal God is your refuge, and underneath are the everlasting arms." (Deuteronomy 33:27)

The Walled Garden

Here is seclusion and peace. Outside the world hurries on, without waiting for me to join again its bustling, pushing and shoving demands of life.

Here I have found a space, to be still, to be calm, to feel the warmth of the sun on my face, to close my eyes and just 'be'.

My heart's burdens, anxious thoughts, concerns for the future, are all left outside with the hurrying world. This is not the place, not today, not right now.

This is a secret place, this garden. Carefully planted blooms in a whole range of different pots, provide a rainbow of colours, red, purple, and orange, blending perfectly, each with its own unique beauty. Nothing clashes here. A gentle breeze brushes across the petals and a soft almost imperceptible fragrance hangs in the air.

Against one wall, a bloom laden Buddleia stands, its purple heads dipping and swaying at the soft touch of the wind. As I sit silent, not moving, watching, blue tits flit in and out of its branches feeding from the bird feeders hanging nearby. Occasional a blackbird or magpie will drop from the wall to pick up seeds that have fallen.

Within these walls, it is so peaceful. I can hear sounds from the road outside. Car doors banging and engines revving, but they seem far away, not loud enough to disturb this precious stillness. Here it is my time to pause; a time to just 'be', a time to just be 'me'.

Here time is standing still. in this place is a meeting with the unseen, unhindered by rush and noise.

So, I sit, but not alone. Someone has come to share this place with me. Unseen but not unknown. We become like two lovers who sit in silence, intimate and comfortable in each other's presence. No words needed, not in this place, no words between me and one who knows my every thought, my every hope, my every dream.

We are known to each other. Here I feel His presence, know His peace. Here I find beauty in both the seen and the unseen, and I sit with Him in stillness. Here I am reassured of love.

This is my treasure in this moment, to be still, to listen, to receive, to know. So, I sit, and rest, in this walled garden. The world outside can wait a little longer.

JESUS
HERE I AM
JUST AS I AM
FINDING YOUR LOVE
IS HERE TOO

♪ ♪ ♪ ♪ ♪ ♪

"It's in Christ that we find out who we are and what we are living for. Long before we first heard of Christ and got our hopes up, he had his eye on us and had designs on us for glorious living, part of the overall purpose he is working out in everything and everyone." (Ephesians 1:11-12 MSG)

The Power of Your Love

I've felt the fire of your Spirit
Burning in my heart
Filling every part
The darkness flees before the light
The victory is won by
The overcoming Son

The power of your love has set me free
And now I'm living to become
All that I can be
I have a future and a hope
Death no longer threatens me
For the power of you love
Has set me free

"So if the Son sets you free, you will be free indeed." (John 8:36)

Open My Eyes

Open my eyes LORD
That I may see
The truth in your word
That is setting me free

Open my eyes LORD
Cause me to hear
Your whispers of love to me
When I draw near

"Draw near to God and He will draw near to you." (James 4:8)

There is a Place

There is a place that I dream of
Where sadness and crying are far away
The sun really shines every morning
And laughter fills the air each day

There is a place that I long for
A place where I no longer have to hide
Where love is the air that I breath in
And where at last I'm free inside

There is a place that I yearn for
I know that it's real; it's here in my heart
I'm living the promise each moment;
I know that this is just the start

All that that this world has to give me
Cannot compare to what is to come
Now all of my life is a pathway
I'm on the way - I'm heading home.

There is a hope deep within me
Certain and real though it's yet to come
Nothing in this world can hold me
I'm on my way - I'm heading home

"And if I go and prepare a place for you, I will come back and take you to be with me that you also may be where I am." (John 14:3)

Father

Father in your love there's such a joy
And peace beyond all measure
Standing in your presence I can see
All that it is that you want me to be
In your love

Father in your love I'm finding
Moments of enduring treasure
And times of resting in security
Now at last I'm learning to be free
Through your love

Silent in wonder
Catching the beat of your heart
Feeling my spirit rise and soar
Touching the glory your holy majesty
Watching and waiting
Not wanting to leave you
Abiding in your eternity

Father in your love I'm trusting
Though I'm often weak and failing
Yet I know that there is victory
In all that you have planned for me
In your love

"...for the Father himself loves you dearly because you love me and believe that I came from God." (John 16:27 New Living Trans.)

Judas

So now the time has come for you to walk away.
You've turned from Me and will not meet my eyes.
The night has fallen fast, the sun is hidden in your life.
Your ears are deaf to hear what is to come.

The depth of love I feel for you, you feel no more.
This love within my heart which bids you come;
And soon the day will wash away the night in which you
hide, and hidden from your sight I will be gone.

How I longed, oh how I longed to draw you near.
To remove the walls dividing us. To drive away your fears.
But your heart was filled with other things
And you just couldn't hear; you couldn't understand.

And now I see you walk away into the night
The world has caught you and held you in it snare
You chose the way which separates us and you cannot see
All you thought that you would want you cannot have
And who is losing?

"As soon as Judas had taken the bread, he went out. And it was night." (John 13:30)

Broken World

Even in a broken world the presence of God can be known for those who wish to search, to know, to be true to what is hidden deep in every human heart, the treasure he has buried there.

"You will seek Me and find Me, when you will search for Me with all your heart." (Jeremiah 29:13)

"He has also set eternity in the hearts of men,.." (Ecclesiastes 3:11)

"One thing you realise as you go through trials is that you can't go all theological; you need a God who is real, who is living, who hears you when you pray and has the power to bring answers!"

Inspire

"None of us should underestimate the influence we have on someone else's life, for good or for bad. While each one alone is accountable for his own life and the choices he makes, yet we can determine that through our own lives we endeavour to inspire in those we know and love a sense of their self-worth and potential, enabling them to enrich their own lives and the lives of others"

"Therefore encourage one another and build each other up, just as in fact you are doing." (1 Thessalonians 5:11)

Reach Out

From "The Life Giver" Musical

Reach out and touch Him
Jesus is looking your way
Receive His mercy and His love
He'll never turn you away.
He can see you in your need
He understands all of your fears
Reach out and touch the Lord
Jesus is here

Reach out and touch Him
He will not judge or condemn
His heart of compassion is beating for you
He's longing to draw you to Him
Let Him heal your aching heart
Melt away sadness and care
Reach out and touch Him
Jesus is here

Reach out and touch Him
There is so much He will give
Healing forgiveness, immeasurable love
All that you need is in Him
His mighty power will break all your chains
He'll set you free, free indeed
Reach out and touch the Lord
Jesus is here

(Luke 8:43-48)

I Lift My Eyes

"No enemy is strong enough
To take me from your grasp
No valley dark or deep enough
And nothing that is past
When fearful thoughts are troubling me
And peace cannot be found
I'll lift my eyes up to the One
In whom my joy is found"

Here I Stand

Here I stand offering my life to You
With empty hands
Not trying to be anything but what I am.
Here I stand

You a here, trusting in Your promises
I know you care
Believing that You died for me
Drives out my fear
You are here

And oh, my heart reaches out for Your love
And the wonder of Your presence
Come wash me clean in the flow of Your grace
That my worship may be holy
And worthy of You Lord.

"Worship the Lord in the beauty of holiness." (Psalm 96:9)

When I Think

When I think about the miracles
You're working in my life
And the promises that every new day brings
I'm so thankful, and my heart begins to rise
From deep inside my spirit starts to sing

When I think about you walking
in this broken world of ours
and your willingness to suffer all our pain
I'm so grateful that you never turned away
Your love was greater than our sin and shame

Perfect Love

There are times when words cannot express
The way you feel deep inside
And prayer is hard
Maybe you've never tried before
To touch the living God
And you've held back from Him
Afraid of what He has in store
But perfect love casts out all fear
His love can wash away your pain
And it's with Jesus that you
Will find peace of mind
He gave His life for you
Can you believe and start again

"There is no fear in love. But perfect love drives out fear, because fear has to do with punishment. The one who fears is not made perfect in love." (1 John 4:18)

Just Come

From Heaven's throne to earth He came
And in a filthy stable lay.
The One who loves and loves us still
Took lowest place in winters chill
That we the guilty ones might rise
Above the storms of broken lives
To sing again, sorrow subdued
To live again in gracious love.

New life He brings, the old has gone.
Hearts newly healed, by God's own Son.
He is the One who saves us from
The sting of death we die alone.
Who else was there to pay such price?
Perfection given in sacrifice
Yet lovingly He calls each one
"I'm here for you today. Just come."

"Come to me all you who are weary and heavy laden and I will give you rest." (Matthew 11:28)

Printed and bound by CPI Group (UK) Ltd, Croydon, CR0 4YY